CW00689851

Parents' Guide

AGE 5–7

Shirley Clarke and Barry Silsby

Illustrated by Sascha Lipscomb

Contents

Hodder Children's Books

The only home learning programme supported by the NCPTA

Introduction

WHO THIS BOOK IS FOR

This book is for parents of children aged from 5 to 7 years. It is based on the National Curriculum and education system of England and Wales, but much of the information will be helpful wherever you live.

THE PURPOSE OF THIS BOOK

❑ There are many daunting decisions to make when your child first starts school, such as what school to choose and what makes a good school. This book provides all the information you will need to be able to make those decisions.

❑ All parents want their children to do well at school and to be happy there.

❑ This book also gives you sound advice about what and how your child will be taught and how to make sure that he or she is supported and happy.

❑ Knowing how to support your child's learning at school can be a worry. This book takes each subject of the National Curriculum and suggests useful ways in which you can help your child at home.

USING THE BOOK

The book is designed to be dipped into. Use the Contents page to find which aspect of your child's education you want to know more about. 'He' and 'she' are used alternately throughout the book but all references apply to children of either sex.

Choosing a school

There are many different types of school and a little knowledge of how they are different will help you in your choice.

DO I WANT TO PAY FOR MY CHILD'S EDUCATION?

Private or independent schools are fee paying. There are many types of private school, from the part-time nursery schools to national institutions. Your local library will give you details.

State schools provide free education. Information about them can also be obtained from your local library or your local education authority. The major differences between private and state schools are as follows:

Private schools	State schools
❏ are fee paying	are free
❏ do not have to employ qualified teachers	must employ qualified teachers
❏ do not have to teach the National Curriculum	must teach the National Curriculum
❏ do not have to take national tests	must take national tests and publish the results
❏ can select children	can select only a small proportion of children (except selective secondary schools)
❏ usually have smaller classes than state schools	can have classes of up to 40, although 30 is more normal

All schools publish a school booklet or prospectus which can be obtained from the school. Page 4 tells you what to look for in a school prospectus.

WHAT AGE GROUP SHOULD I CHOOSE?

At ages 5 - 7 years, the following types of school are available. Often these schools take younger children, sometimes from 3+ years if there is a nursery included on the premises.

❏ **Infant schools** cater for children up to 7 years old, after which they transfer to a junior school.

❏ **First schools** cater for children up to 8 years old, after which they transfer to a middle school.

❏ **Primary schools** cater for children up to 11 years old, after which they transfer to a secondary school.

It is unlikely that you will find both infant and first schools in the same area because local education authorities usually decide to follow one type of organisation or the other.

HOW IS THE SCHOOL FUNDED AND RUN?

All schools have a board of governors which ensures that the school is run correctly. The governors are lay people who are interested in education. State schools are of three types:

❏ **County** or **local authority** schools receive their funding from the local education authority, who are also responsible for the structure of the building.

❏ **Aided** schools receive most of their funding from the local education authority but a proportion comes from other sources. Typically, these are church schools although a charitable foundation could be providing the funding. Aided schools are responsible for their own buildings.

❏ **Grant maintained** schools are funded directly by the government and are responsible for the complete running of the school.

WHICH SCHOOL SHOULD I CHOOSE?

Generally, the best school to choose is the one which feels right for you once you have visited and read about it. However, there are some basic questions you might ask yourself:

❑ *Do I want my child to receive instruction in a particular religious creed?*

If so, you need to choose an aided school of the denomination you favour.

❑ *Do I want my child to attend a small school?*

Generally, first or infant schools will be smaller than primary schools in a given area. Be careful however, as some first/infant schools are very large.

❑ *Do I want my child to stay in the same school until she goes to secondary school?*

Only a primary school can offer continuous education until age 11.

❑ *Does it matter how far away from home the school is?*

If you choose a school far away from where you live your child is going to have to travel a long distance to maintain friendships. Consider how your child is going to travel to or from school, and how easily you can get to her if, for example, she is ill at school. Feeling part of the local community might also be important to you.

❑ *What should I do once I have found a school I am interested in?*

You need to arrange a visit. Phone the school to ask for an appointment and ask for a school prospectus to be sent to you before your visit. Try to arrange the visit during the school day at least 3 weeks after the term has started. In this way, you will be able to watch the children at work in the classrooms and there should be plenty of work on display for you to look at. Arrange child-care if necessary. You really cannot concentrate on choosing a school if you are trying to look after your child(ren) at the same time.

WHAT TO LOOK FOR IN A SCHOOL PROSPECTUS

Read the prospectus before you visit. Is it easy to read? Does it give you a 'feel' for the school? Look at the school's assessment results (see page 14), but remember that there is more to a school than academic results. Has the school made an obvious effort to project itself?

Just two warnings, however:

❑ There are legal requirements for school prospectuses which are constantly changing. Some of the information required by law is difficult to make 'user-friendly'.

❑ Schools have to pay for the printing of the prospectus out of the same budget as they buy school books and pay staff. A slick multi-coloured booklet might look the best, but this is beyond the means of most small schools. It is what is said in the prospectus that is important, not necessarily how it is produced.

WHAT TO LOOK FOR WHEN YOU VISIT A SCHOOL

❑ *How does the school feel as you walk around?*

It is sometimes difficult to explain why, but different schools feel different as you walk around. Is there a welcoming atmosphere? Do the children seem happy? Is there a good working atmosphere? Do you feel comfortable? Do you think this is the type of environment your child would be happy in?

❑ *How are the children acting?*

In lessons, are they getting on with their work, but not looking frightened or seeming too quiet? Are they polite as you meet them around the school? Are they obviously proud of their work? Do they seem to be supporting, rather than quarrelling with, each other?

❑ *How are the staff acting?*

Be careful with this one. Teachers work intensively and tend not to like interruptions when talking to children. Bearing this in mind, are they welcoming? How do they talk to the children?

❏ *Look at the work on display*

Look carefully at displays. There should be plenty of bright, stimulating displays in the school. They should also be mainly of children's work, not just posters and photographs. Does the work obviously get better as the children get older and can you tell the things the class are studying from the work on display?

❏ *Look at the class facilities*

Does each class have a sink and art area? Does it have a computer? Are there obvious areas in the classroom, such as a book corner? What are the facilities for play? Does the classroom seem well equipped?

Look at the school's facilities

What are the facilities for sports and games? Does the school have a library? What are the play facilities like? Are there extra rooms or areas for group-work?

Look at the building in general

Is the interior in good repair and the furniture well looked after? (The school has control of the outside of the building only if it is grant maintained.) Has the school taken appropriate steps to ensure security?

Ask questions

Schools have changed since you were at primary school, so do not be frightened to ask questions. A good school will be pleased to make sure you understand how the school is run. Your questions will vary according to who is taking you around. If children show you around, remember that they are a great source of what it is like to be part of the school, but not too hot on the intricacies of the National Curriculum. You should get a chance to talk to the head or a senior teacher. Ask him or her about anything that is unclear to you. Here are some questions you might like to ask:

✧ How are children rewarded for good work?

✧ Is there a school policy on discipline?

✧ Are there opportunities for parents to help in school?

✧ What provision is there for children who need extra help with their work?

✧ What extra-curricular activities does the school offer?

✧ Is there a Parent-Teacher Association (or equivalent)?

Above all, enjoy your visit. If you don't, it is unlikely that your child will enjoy the school.

YOUR LEGAL RIGHTS AND WHAT TO DO ONCE YOU HAVE CHOSEN A SCHOOL

Legally, a school place has to be provided for every child from the school term after their fifth birthday. In fact, most schools take in children when they are younger than this. Find out from the school prospectus or the local education authority at what age the school you are interested in admits children.

Filling out the form

You will be required to fill out a form. This might be a form from the local authority, the school's own form, or sometimes both. You may legally express a preference for a school that you like. Provided there is a place available, the school must offer it to you. However, if the school has more applications than places, some children will be refused. It is then up to the local education authority to find an alternative school place for these children.

What if the school I want refuses me a place?

This is not a judgement on you or your child. It usually just means the school is too popular. In this case, the school must apply its admissions policy, which is published in the prospectus, and inform you in writing why your child has been refused a place. The local education authority should then offer you a place in an alternative school.

The first thing you should do is to go and look at the school you have been offered. You might be pleasantly surprised. Once you have done this, you should consider the following choices:

❏ To accept the alternative school. In this case, you need do nothing further.

❏ To accept the alternative school but ask for your name to be placed on the waiting list for the school of your first choice. In this case, your child will attend the alternative school until a place becomes available at your first-choice school. This can cause more difficulties, however, as you then have to decide whether to move your child mid-term to a new school where he has to settle in and make new friends again.

❏ To appeal against the decision to refuse your child a place. This is a procedure set up to allow parents to appeal to an independent panel. The first step is to fill out an appeals form which you can get from your local education office. Once this has been processed, you will be asked to go to a local place where the appeals will be heard. You can take a friend with you if you wish. The procedure is quite informal. The representative of the local education authority or the school will be asked why a place was refused, and then you will be asked why you think your child should be offered a place. It is a good idea to have thought about this and written down a few notes beforehand. State your reasons simply and clearly. Good things to mention are how easy the school is to reach from your house (or how difficult an alternative

school is), friends or family attending the school, and any links such as a local play group. At the end of the appeal, you will be asked whether you have anything else to say and when the panel will let you know its decision. This rarely takes more than a few days. The panel's decision is binding, whichever way it decides.

Nursery Vouchers

At the time of writing, the government is aiming to introduce vouchers. These can be used to purchase education for all children in the year before they are 5, in private nurseries, playgroups, state nurseries and schools. However, they can only be used for one type of education. You cannot have your child at school part-time in the mornings and at a playgroup in the afternoon, both paid for by the voucher. A different system of nursery provision may be introduced if there is a change of government.

You have to apply for nursery vouchers and you should look out for the government's publicity campaign to tell you when to apply. It is very important that you do apply for vouchers. If your child is already at school, or about to attend school, he might well be refused admission if you do not have a voucher at the appropriate time.

Preparing for school

If your child has been to a nursery or playgroup, she will already understand a lot about school. However, children who have only been at home need to be introduced to school-type behaviour, which is different from the way they behave at home.

Good schools will help you with the process by arranging visits and gradually introducing the child to school in the first term. At first your child might stay at school for only an hour, gradually building up time until she is at school full-time.

HELPING YOUR CHILD PREPARE FOR SCHOOL

❏ **Take every opportunity to visit schools with your child and talk about schooling with her.** This doesn't have to be the school she is going to. Visiting the schools of friends' or family's children, schools which are having open days, or just walking past a school in session (avoid the beginning/end of the school day as this can be quite hectic) and talking about what is happening inside are all good preparation.

❏ **Talk positively about school.** Tell your child what will happen. Tell her that you will not be with her at school but reassure her that you will be back to pick her up at the end of the session. Tell her that if she wants anything at all, she should tell the teacher or any adult on the school staff.

❏ **Get your child to mix with other children as much as possible.** At school she will need to know how to share. This means sharing things such as toys, books and equipment and also sharing time with the teacher or other adults. Sharing does not come easily to children and you need to talk to them positively about it.

❏ **Encourage your child in school-type play.** This does not just mean playing at reading or writing; include painting, making things, looking carefully at pictures and talking about them and listening to a story. Encourage your child to use instruments such as magnifying glasses, scissors, and tape recorders. Let her play with a cheap calculator and encourage her to count things.

❏ Make school-type activities a pleasant experience between you and your child. Do read to her, but choose the time carefully. Don't do it when her favourite television programme is on. Bedtime is a good time for reading together, particularly if it is a 'treat' which extends the time before the child is expected to go to sleep. It is important that fathers take part in this activity as well as mothers to show that reading is a pleasant activity for males and females. Try to include the following activities as well:

⬦ counting (when going up and down stairs, when shopping)

⬦ talking about time ('morning', 'evening', days of the week) and what you commonly do then ('on Fridays we visit Grandma')

⬦ rhymes (especially traditional nursery rhymes)

⬦ recognising words about the home (eg 'Corn Flakes', *Radio Times*)

⬦ recognising her own name (if you write it for her, use a capital to begin and then use lower case [small] letters)

❑ Try to make your child as independent as possible when dealing with clothing. She will need to remove or undo clothing to go to the toilet, and get undressed for P.E. She will need to be able to put on and do up, undo and take off her coat. She will have to put on and take off school clothing such as painting aprons. You can help by not making things too difficult for her. Elasticated waistbands and velcro fasteners are far easier to handle than buttons, zip fasteners and long laces.

❑ Try to help your child to be careful with her possessions. She will need to look after her own things and will be expected to tidy up in the classroom. You can help by marking or sewing name-tapes on to all her possessions and clothes and by encouraging her to be tidy at home. This will help you as well as your child's entry to school.

Tips about helping your child once she is at school can be found in Chapter 5, 'Ensuring that your child is happy at school'.

An overview of the infant or first school

Infant schools (and infant departments of primary schools) or first schools will provide many different experiences for your child. They will also cover up to 3 different educational stages. Children do not have to go to school until the term after they are 5. Once your child is 5 he is described as of 'statutory school age'.

However, many schools take children as young as 3 and most take in 4-year-olds. Legal requirements for school children (that is the subjects they must study) only apply to children of statutory age. Therefore what is taught to the younger children (often called 'early years' or 'reception' children) can be different from what is taught to children once they are 5. Between the ages of 5 and 7, children are described as being in Key Stage 1. What they have to be taught is laid down in the National Curriculum. If your child is in a first school, some of the oldest children will be in Key Stage 2, which includes children from the school year they are 8 until the school year they are 11.

The following examples attempt to show the types of activities which your child might experience on entering school, and those which he would be expected to develop by the end of Key Stage 1, when he will be in Year 2.

TYPICAL EXPERIENCES FOR YOUR CHILD OVER ONE WEEK

(These are typical activities and ways in which a typical child of that age would respond to them. Remember, however, that all children develop differently and this should in no way be used as a 'check-list'. Reading reports and talking to your child's teacher are far better ways of checking on his progress.)

Activity	At age 5 (reception or early years class)	At age 7 (Year 2 class)
Writing	Will make a book by choosing, or being encouraged, to work in the writing area. Writing will probably consist of a few letters, but the child will know what it says.	Writing will probably be the result of a task set by the teacher related to the work going on in the class. The writing will be readable and will be arranged sensibly (beginning, middle, ending) with most simple words spelled correctly. Sentences will mainly have capital letters and full stops.
Art	Pictures will probably have strange colouring (blue hair etc).	Illustration will have correct colouring and suit the writing.

Activity	At age 5 (reception or early years class)	At age 7 (Year 2 class)

Reading

Will 'read' independently in the book corner or to another child or adult. Will read a book he knows well by memory or by telling the story rather than reading it. Will be able to recognise a few words.

Will have specific reading sessions in class. Will be able to read most books at the appropriate level guided by the teacher, and some words from all reading matter. Knows when a word makes sense in a sentence and when it doesn't. Can work out simple unknown words by sounding out.

Mathematics

Will measure out liquids while playing in the water tray and find out the answers to simple questions such as 'how many times can you fill the small container from the big one'. Will record results by drawing or talking to the teacher.

Will be able to solve problems such as 'find a container that holds exactly a litre' and will be able to record in his own way.

Science

Will plant seeds in the class garden or in pots in the classroom and watch them grow. Will read stories about seeds growing and will talk with the teacher about how seeds grow. The class might make a display about seeds. The highlight, if the plant is edible, will be eating it!

Will perform an experiment, alone or as part of a group, to see what conditions are necessary for seeds to live. Will keep regular notes and drawings during the experiment and will come to a conclusion at the end. The highlight, if the plant is edible, will still be eating it!

Activity	At age 5 (reception or early years class)	At age 7 (Year 2 class)
Art	Will paint on an easel using thick lines and colour. Will paint a subject suggested by the teacher related to the topic being studied in the class. The picture will tend to be simple and unrealistic. Will look at a group of pictures and say which one he likes best. Might give a reason why.	Can use more refined techniques including simple self-mixed water colour. Paintings/drawings will be more realistic, particularly when drawing from life (eg drawing a water creature obtained while pond-dipping). When given two representations of similar scenes by different artists, will be able to notice differences between the techniques and say which one he prefers.

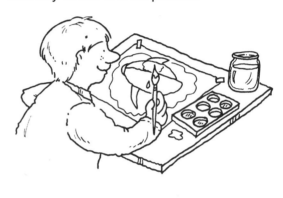

Activity	At age 5	At age 7
PE	Will run, jump with both feet and make various movements when asked.	Will be able to work with a partner to produce a sequence of movements with a distinct beginning and end.

Activity	At age 5	At age 7
History	Will talk about his own family and relative ages, often drawing pictures of Gran, Mum, me, baby cousin etc. Will talk about the past and the future with the teacher. Will be told stories, some factual, some fictional, about things that happened long, long ago.	Will examine old-fashioned objects or photographs and compare them with objects, people or places today. Will try to imagine why there are differences and why there are similarities, mainly in discussion with the teacher and the rest of the class. Will read stories of famous people.

A WORD ABOUT PLAY

Children will often come home from school and tell you they have been 'playing all day'. This concerns some parents, who rightly say that children go to school to learn. However, there is a difference between ordinary or unstructured play, such as that which takes place at home or in the playground, and structured play which takes place in the classroom.

Teachers spend a great deal of time planning structured play activities so that children will learn the skills necessary for future, more formal work-type activities.

EXAMPLES OF STRUCTURED PLAY:

❑ Children might feel that they have been playing by digging in the sand or pouring water and making boats in the water tray. The teacher knows that by the equipment s/he has provided and the task s/he set the child, that the child is in fact learning the basics for later work in capacity or volume (Maths) or in flotation (Physics) or hydraulics (Technology).

❑ Playing shops will introduce the skills of measure and money (Maths), of role play (playing at being different characters such as the shopkeeper and customers, and finding out how they interact) and communication (Drama and English).

Play is very important in learning. The amount of overt play will decrease as the child gets older, but it will not disappear altogether.

The National Curriculum

The National Curriculum sets out what children must be taught at school. It consists of 10 subjects:

- ✧ **English**
- ✧ **Mathematics**
- ✧ **Science**
- ✧ **Information Technology**
- ✧ **Design Technology**
- ✧ **History**
- ✧ **Geography**
- ✧ **Art**
- ✧ **Music**
- ✧ **Physical Education**

Teachers are also required to teach Religious Education, but there is no National Curriculum for this. Instead, representatives of local religious groups meet to recommend a syllabus.

Each subject of the National Curriculum sets out what must be taught for the different age ranges. As stated earlier, children aged 5 to 7 are taught the Key Stage 1 sections.

WHAT ARE THE LEGAL REQUIREMENTS?

According to the Education Act of 1988, children are entitled to be taught a range of subjects, and for there to be a good balance between them.

Although what must be taught is a legal requirement, how teachers teach it is up to the school to decide. So, for example, children have to learn to add numbers, but different schools often have different Maths schemes, with different activities for getting children to understand how to add.

You can buy a copy of the National Curriculum from most bookshops or from HMSO Publications Centre - Telephone 0171 873 9090

WHAT IS CONTAINED IN EACH SUBJECT?

There are 2 sections: The **Programmes of Study** and the **Level Descriptions**. Here is a simple explanation for each:

PROGRAMMES OF STUDY

This is a list of what children must be taught. It is split up into different sections. The English Programmes of Study, for instance, are divided into the following sections:

Speaking and Listening

'Pupils should be given opportunities to talk for a range of purposes, including:
telling stories, both real and imagined; imaginative play and drama; reading and listening to nursery rhymes and poetry ...'

Reading

'Pupils should be given extensive experience of children's literature. They should read on their own, with others and to the teacher, from a range of genres that include stories, poetry, plays and picture books ...'

Writing

'Pupils should be taught to write with confidence, fluency and accuracy. They should be taught to differentiate between print and pictures, to understand the connections between speech and writing ...'

THE LEVEL DESCRIPTIONS

Each Attainment Target (or aspect) of each subject is divided into 8 paragraphs, describing the standards of attainment, or what you would typically expect children to be able to achieve in each subject at different levels between the ages of 4 and 16. The levels are listed from 1 to 8 with Level 1 at the beginning and Level 8 at the end. Each level lists skills and abilities which are found in the Programmes of Study. The average 7-year-old is likely to be achieving Level 2.

END OF KEY STAGE TESTS

At the end of Year 2 (the end of Key Stage 1), all children in England and Wales have to take some written and oral tests for English and Maths, unless they have severe learning needs. These tests are known as SATs (standard assessment tasks) or 'national tests'.

The tests are written by experts and marked by the teachers in the school. It is the local authority's job to make sure that all teachers apply the same standard. It does this by collecting work and by visiting the school and watching the teacher administer the tests. There is more advice about tests on page 22.

❏ *When will my child be doing the tests and how long will they last?*

Children do the tests at any time from the middle of the Spring term to the middle of the Summer term. Teachers need this length of time to be able to organise the tests, because they often have to talk to each child individually as part of the test.

The actual time your child will spend on the tests will total 3 – 5 hours.

❏ *How will I know how well my child has done?*

The teacher marks the test according to a standard system, which will result in your child being given a level for his English achievement and another level for Mathematics achievement. The range of levels possible is:
W (working towards Level 1), Level 1, Level 2, Level 3 and Level 4. Your child's end of year report will show these levels.

❏ *What exactly will my child have to do for the tests?*

The tests consist of a number of tasks, which look very similar to the child's normal work. Examples of these tasks are: writing a story, reading to the teacher, answering questions about a story and filling in some Maths worksheets.

❏ *Will my child be worried about the tests?*

Teachers work very hard at making children feel relaxed and happy during the tests:

✧ They organise them so that they are not all doing the tests at once, so the classroom feels 'normal', although there is one whole class comprehension test for children who are thought to be achieving at Level 2.

✧ They tell them to just do their best and not to worry, because their best is good enough.

✧ They make sure that children who can't read or write very well are not made to feel a failure; they let them have a go then tell them to stop, and praise them for what they have done.

✧ Children can have questions about Maths read out to them, so they have a fair chance to show their ability.

✧ There are special faciltities for disabled children or children with special needs.

Teachers often say how much children seem to enjoy the tests!

When your child starts school

Children are naturally apprehensive about their first day at school, however carefully they have been prepared for it. Although some show no signs of anxiety at all, others find it very difficult and a small number become upset. Whether they remain upset depends very much on how you handle the situation.

Parents, particularly with a first child, often find the first day just as traumatic. Any primary head will tell you that far more tears are shed by mothers than by children. This is fine as long as it happens outside, away from the child after you have said goodbye. Nothing will make a first day more difficult for a child than an obviously upset parent.

The first day will normally be shorter than usual so that children do not have to cope with too many hours at first. It is likely that the children will be brought in in groups so there are some children who are already settled and ready to help newcomers. Most schools will also make sure there are plenty of staff around the new class at the beginning. Some will use older brothers and sisters already in the school.

❏ *What should I do before I take my child to school?*

Make sure you know when to arrive, what time you will be picking your child up and what she needs for the first day. If the school has a uniform, make sure your child is wearing it. Make sure her possessions are named and clothes and shoes are comfortable and easy to undo. Remember, school is a messy place, so don't send your child in best clothes or tell her to keep clean.

❏ *What do I do when I take my child to school?*

Take your child to the classroom. Help her hang up her coat and see her into the classroom. Some schools let parents stay a while, but most like them to leave as soon as possible to avoid upsets. Say goodbye to your child, tell her you are going and that you will be back.

❏ *What do I do if she gets upset?*

Still do the same, and go. Schools are very experienced at dealing with upsets. Once your child becomes involved in the many exciting activities, she will forget about being upset. The school has your telephone number, but it is highly unlikely it will need to use it.

❏ *What do I do if she doesn't get upset?*

Many parents take this as an insult, particularly if their child doesn't even say goodbye! Take it as a compliment and go!

HOW TO FIND OUT HOW YOUR CHILD IS PROGRESSING

School reports

It is a statutory requirement that you receive a report of your child's progress at the end of each school year. Each school can produce its own style of report, but it must include information on the following:

- ✧ Progress in all the National Curriculum subjects
- ✧ General progress, such as attitude to work, behaviour and social abilities
- ✧ Attendance

❏ *What about levels of attainment?*

National Curriculum levels only have to be given, by law, at the end of the Key Stages; that is, at the end of Year 2 and Year 6.

At this time, teachers also have to decide a level for each child for English, Maths and Science. These are given to you alongside the test levels.

❏ *Why is it necessary to have two sets of levels?*

One set of levels is based on the tests, but the other levels are based on the standard of your child's ongoing work in the classroom. These are called **Teacher Assessment** levels or TA. Your child might have a higher or lower level for Teacher Assessment compared with the test level, because children sometimes do better or worse at a test than expected.

❏ *Will the report tell me whether my child is average, below average or above average?*

Most teachers indicate in the report how your child compares with the average child. However, if you don't feel sure, simply ask the teacher at

the Open Day which is normally held towards the end of each term (see below).

❏ *What if I want to discuss the report with the teacher?*

When you receive your child's report, you should be offered an appointment to discuss it at the Open Day. If you are satisfied with the report, you do not need to take this up (although a note to the class teacher expressing your satisfaction would be much appreciated). If there is anything about the report you do not understand, you should take up the offer of an interview.

OPEN DAYS

The purpose of Open Days or Open Evenings is to give you a chance to see your child's work and to talk about her progress.

The Open Day at the end of the Summer term is the time when you usually receive your child's progress report, although some schools send them to the parents. Your child's teacher will explain the report to you and answer any questions you may have.

At the Open Day or Open Evening:
- ✧ Do look carefully at your child's work.
- ✧ It is impolite to look at other children's work if it is in personal books or folders, but do look carefully at the displays in the classroom. These will give you a very good idea how your child's work compares with others.
- ✧ If you are worried or confused about anything, mention this at the beginning of the meeting. If it is not a quick matter, it might be best to make an appointment for a longer talk.
- ✧ Try not to over-run. Most teachers can only allow 5-10 minutes per child. If you have more to discuss, ask for another appointment.
- ✧ Teachers enjoy hearing about things you are pleased with.

❏ *How much of my child's work should I expect to see by the end of a year?*

Much of the work done by children in the infants is practical, with nothing written on paper by the children. This can make you think that your child

has not got much to show for her year's work, but you need to remember the well-researched importance of practical activities as a way of firmly establishing vital understanding of English and Maths in young children.

Here are some examples of practical work your child is likely to do and what he or she will be learning:

Practical activity	What your child is learning
Reading to the teacher	Learning to read
A 'big book' session: the teacher reads a giant book to the class, pointing out the words as she goes and talking about the words	Learning about reading, spelling, grammar and punctuation
Playing a Maths game	Learning to count, add, subtract, multiply or divide
Seeing which container holds the most in the sand tray	Learning about the measurement of liquids
Emptying a jar of small cubes and grouping them in tens, then counting the total	Learning how to count and the place value of numbers

The written work you will see is likely to be:

- ✧ handwriting practice
- ✧ story writing
- ✧ diary writing
- ✧ writing about Science, Maths or other subjects
- ✧ writing produced on a word processor
- ✧ some written Maths, not necessarily sums, but often your child's own recording of numbers and calculations

What should I do if, at any time during the year, I am worried about my child's progress?

❑ Firstly, talk to your child about how she thinks she is getting on at school. Ask if she enjoys school and if she finds anything too difficult or too easy. Make this discussion low key, or you might worry your child unnecessarily.

❑ If you are still concerned about your child's work or behaviour, the class teacher should be the first contact. If s/he feels it necessary, s/he will often refer you on to another more senior member of staff. This could be a senior teacher, a deputy head or the headteacher, depending on the school's procedures. However, problems need time to sort out so don't try to talk to the teacher while s/he is teaching. Ask for an appointment after school. If the matter is very urgent, then go to the school office and explain the situation. Most headteachers will agree to see parents at short notice in an emergency.

❑ At the meeting, say clearly what you are worried about, asking if there is anything you can do to help. Wait and see what the teacher has to say. It is highly likely that your concerns can be easily dealt with, either by the teacher explaining more about the reason for the type of work your child is doing, or by the teacher showing that you have given him or her important information about how your child feels, which s/he will now act on.

❑ If the problem is not solved easily, you might well want to talk to the headteacher or a senior member of staff. Ask for an appointment at the school office. Many schools also have a teacher designated to support children with special needs. This teacher is called the **special educational needs co-ordinator** (SENCO for short). The term 'special needs' is used to describe a wide range of situations, from children who find work too difficult or too easy to children who are undergoing emotional difficulties. Sencos are often highly skilled and approachable people, and most will offer advice in a very friendly way. If you would like to talk to such a person, make an appointment at the school office in the usual way. A word of warning, though. Most Sencos are also class teachers who do not have time available during the school day, so you might have to wait for an appointment.

Ensuring that your child is happy at school

Most children are perfectly happy at school. However, from time to time, things might happen that make your child unhappy. Common symptoms are not wanting to go to school on certain days, frequent complaints of tummy aches or general unhappiness when asked about school. (Don't confuse this with the 'all right' syndrome. Some children will chat happily about their experiences at school. However, when asked about school most children reply in monosyllables such as 'all right' or 'fine' or 'OK'. This is perfectly normal!)

Try to tell your child that he has to go to school and that if he will tell you what is wrong, you can help him deal with it. Usually, the answer is to talk to one of the school staff referred to in the previous section. Remember that the staff also need information. If their intervention does not solve the problem after a week or so, go back and tell them.

The following are suggestions about how you might help your child with some difficult situations.

MAKING FRIENDS

When it comes to making friends, children are usually best left alone. The following strategies are useful, however:

❑ Don't be over-anxious. Children make friends naturally, but if you are anxious, your child will sense this and feel restricted.

❑ Don't censor friendships. Welcome all your child's friends. Children often befriend children we see as less than desirable. This is their way of finding out about friendship.

❑ Encourage your child to invite children home to play, and allow him to visit his friends as well.

❑ Allow your child to invite friends on some family outings.

❑ Encourage your child to join clubs and organisations out of school to widen his circle of friends.

❑ If your child is really unhappy about friendships at school, tell his teacher. S/he might be able to help and will certainly be able to give an unbiased view.

WHEN FRIENDS FALL OUT

Friends sometimes fall out and this is devastating to a child. What can you do to help?

❑ Give it time. Fall-outs are usually only short-lived

❑ Be sympathetic, but don't criticise the friend. He is likely to be a best friend again in the future!

❑ Don't get involved with the other child's parents unless you know them very well. Children make up quarrels easily, adults don't.

❑ Encourage your child to have a wide circle of friends so that he has others to play with.

❏ Children often fall out with a single member of a group of friends and then pick on that person. Encourage your child not to get involved in this. If he does, it will certainly be his turn to be picked on soon.

BULLYING

Children often get into arguments and disagreements and these may be described as bullying. The first thing to decide is whether this really is bullying or just an argument or one-off difficulty.

Bullying …
❏ takes place over a long period of time
❏ can involve hurting someone physically, constantly being nasty to someone, stealing from someone or insisting on 'presents', vandalising or destroying possessions
❏ causes personality changes in the victim
❏ can make the child afraid to tell anyone, including you
❏ is very serious and must be dealt with

If you suspect your child is being bullied, contact the school immediately. If it continues, go back again. Most schools have policies to deal with bullying and take it very seriously. However, be

prepared for the school's view to be different from yours after the incidents have been investigated.

BEHAVING BADLY AT SCHOOL

Children sometimes behave badly at school. Good schools will have a discipline or behaviour policy and will ensure that parents are informed and involved well before a problem is serious.

The first thing a teacher will do when a child misbehaves is speak to him about what he did; first, when it happens, then privately afterwards. Teachers try to understand what has caused the problem and question children to see whether it was the child's fault or due to some other factor, such as another child's influence, an accident or a misunderstanding.

Schools have various punishments for children who continue to misbehave. These include:
✧ sending them to work in another class
✧ keeping them in at playtime or lunchtime
✧ telling them to report to a senior teacher

The most severe punishment is exclusion from school. This can be for up to 45 days a year, although it is usually for 2 or 3 days at first. This sanction is only used in very extreme circumstances and parents would certainly know of the possibility of exclusion well before it happens.

All children get into trouble from time to time and you should not worry about odd instances. However, if your child seems to be in trouble constantly, you should check this out with the class teacher. If your child has been misbehaving, the way to deal with it is by co-operating with the school. When parents and school pursue a logical, united approach, most difficulties can be overcome. The following are some ways to approach bad behaviour with your child.

❑ Children in trouble often blame other children for leading them astray. Point out that your child knows what is right and that he can say 'no'. 'He told me to do it' is not an excuse.

❑ If you want to punish your child at home as well, discuss this with the school first. As a general rule, misbehaviour at school is best dealt with by appropriate punishment at school and parental disapproval of the child's behaviour at home.

❑ Positive ways of dealing with bad behaviour are often more effective than punishment. For example, a child who behaves badly at playtime might have a card which is completed by the teacher on duty each day, saying how he has behaved. Each week, the child must aim to get more and more 'Good' playtimes until they are always good.

❑ Moving classes within a school is rarely the answer, although a change of school is sometimes effective. This should not be necessary if the school and parents can work together.

❑ Physical punishment is illegal in schools and is the least effective of all forms of punishment.

FINDING SCHOOL TOO DIFFICULT

Some children have great difficulty with all school work. Others just have difficulty in a specific area. In either case, the school should notice and alert you. However, if you have any concerns, talk to the class teacher, headteacher, or special needs co-ordinator about it. Very often this will set your mind at rest. If your child still has difficulties,

however, there are many things a school can do.

⬦ Children can be given special work in class by their teacher.

⬦ An assistant can come into class to help your child with his work.

⬦ Your child could be taken out of class by a specialist teacher for some of the time.

⬦ Children can attend a special unit for some of the time.

All of these things depend on funding. Some local education authorities provide extra help in the form of specialist teachers. Others leave it to the school to pay. In cases of severe learning problems, a school or a parent can ask for a child to be assessed for a **statement of educational need**. This is a long consultative process which requires reports on the child by the parents, the school and an **educational psychologist**. These reports go to a panel which recommends whether the child is to be given extra help and what this help should consist of. If the panel agrees to give help, a **statement of educational need** is drafted in the child's name. Statements must be funded, are enforceable and have to be reviewed annually.

FINDING SCHOOL TOO EASY

Many children say work is easy. Often the product does not live up to the boast! However, if your child does find all work too easy, it is worth discussing this with the class teacher or headteacher. (The special needs co-ordinator might also be involved if your child is so academically able that he needs special work).

The most likely result would be that targets set for your child will be higher than before. This means that the work set for your child will be harder so that it is more challenging and hopefully more interesting.

TAKING TESTS

Your child's teacher will encourage the children to do their best at tests, but will also tell the children not to worry about them. If children feel anxious or panicky about tests, it can lead to a drop in confidence, a fall back in the standard of their work and a poor test result.

If your child is anxious, it may be best not to mention the tests. If your child mentions them, show interest, but make it clear that as long as your child does his best, you will be pleased with him. If you feel that your child would benefit from help to prepare for the SATs, Hodder Home Learning publish two books of practice tests for 7-year-olds, *English Tests* and *Maths Tests*. These can be presented to your child in a relaxed way which boosts his confidence about the real thing.

The test results will *not* affect which class your child goes to next. The purpose of the tests is to produce national statistical information about how well schools are doing, not to decide what should happen to individual children. There is therefore no point in pushing your child to get a high level, a move which is likely to make him unnecessarily anxious.

GETTING ON WITH TEACHERS

Generally children begin by being apprehensive about their teachers and end up idolising them to the extent that the teacher's 'words of wisdom' are quoted constantly at home. However, there will always be a favourite and some children find

it hard to accept an alternative. There can also be personality clashes, as there can everywhere. If you find that your child is having difficulty getting along with his class teacher, try the following.

- ◇ If it is the start of the year, give it time. Teachers are always fiercer with a new class until they get to know them.
- ◇ Talk to your child about different personalities (use friends as examples) and explain that people cannot all be the same.
- ◇ Always talk positively about your child's teacher.
- ◇ Find out *why* (is he always in trouble? Can't get work finished?)
- ◇ Make an appointment with the teacher (don't take your child) and talk openly about it. This might solve the problem, or at least give you an insight into it.
- ◇ Help in your child's class. This might make him feel more secure, and it will help you see how he acts.

How to help your child with the National Curriculum

Your child will have a rich education during her hours at school. Although you can enhance her learning by doing many of the activities suggested below, it is important that home does not become an extension of school. Children need to relax and play in their leisure time or they are likely to become anxious or nervous. Even when you are reading a book with your child, it is important not to keep correcting, but to enjoy the experience together.

On the following pages, we take each of the National Curriculum subjects in turn and give ideas for ways in which you can help your child.

ENGLISH

English is divided into three equal parts; **Speaking and Listening**, **Reading** and **Writing**.

Speaking and Listening

❑ Talk with your child about things you are doing together.

❑ Explain new words and phrases and give your child words to use if she is struggling with an explanation.

❑ Encourage your child to ask questions and to listen to the answers.

❑ Send your child with 'messages' to other members of the family.

❑ Learn nursery rhymes and favourite short poems together.

❑ Play memory games with your child. An example is shown below.

❑ Encourage your child's 'dramatic streak'. Particularly encourage role play, when you each take on different characters in a game or made-up sketch.

❑ Ask your child to describe visits she has made without you.

Memory game
'I went to market'.

The first player says 'I went to market and bought some (for example) apples' and mimes eating an apple. The second says 'I went to market and bought some apples and some sweets', and so on, building up a list of purchases. The game finishes when the child is unable to remember the whole list of articles. At first you might have to do all the mimes, although these can be left out to make the game more challenging. Remember how many articles your child got to and try to beat that score next time.

Reading

The most important thing you can do to help your child at school is to read to and with her. However, it is not your job to teach her to read, but rather to support her in her learning.

❑ Reading to children is important even when they can read themselves. Choose a relaxed time such as bedtime.

- ❑ Read *with* your child, don't expect to hear her read, as her teacher hears her at school. Use the 'Shared Reading' technique shown below.

- ❑ Don't force your child to read. This is the quickest way to turn children off reading

- ❑ Don't be surprised if your child often re-reads a favourite book. This is quite normal and is very supportive for the child.

- ❑ Accept the fact that at times your child will choose a book you think is too easy. This is fine as long as it doesn't always happen.

- ❑ If your child is reading to you, don't over-correct, particularly if she is getting the meaning of the story right.

- ❑ If your child does read a word wrongly, try asking questions such as 'Does — — make sense there?' rather than saying 'No' or 'Wrong'.

- ❑ If your child is stuck on a word, tell it to her.

- ❑ If either of you is tired, stop reading.

Shared reading

Shared reading is a supportive way of reading with a child. It allows you to tackle more challenging books (with you reading most of the texts) and old, loved books (with the child doing most of the work).

- ✧ Read at a relaxed time when both of you are calm.

- ✧ Begin by always reading a new book to your child. Then talk about the book. Ask questions such as 'Which character did you like best?' 'Were you surprised when — —- happened?'

- ✧ Next, ask your child to join in with you as you re-read. For a time, she is likely to read one beat behind you, but as confidence increases you will be reading in unison.

- ✧ Once your child is confident (or if she asks you to), stop reading and allow her to read on alone.

- ✧ Join in again if your child begins to stumble or if she asks you to.

- ✧ In future, ask if your child wants to read alone or if you should read together.

WRITING

- ❑ Encourage your child in writing-type play (making books, playing schools, writing plays etc)

- ❑ Always praise your child for any 'writing' she might do, even if it is not 'real' writing.

- ❑ Ask your child to read you what she has written. She will be able to do so, even if she has done pretend or scribble writing.

- ❑ It is always best for your child to try to write for herself rather than you writing something for her to copy.

- ❑ If you do write for your child, never write all in capitals. Use small letters (lower case) except for the beginning of a sentence or the beginning of a name.

- ❑ When your child is beginning to write, encourage her to sign birthday cards and 'thank you' letters. As she becomes more proficient, get her to write her own.

- ❑ If your child is worried about spellings, get her to put in the initial letter and a dash for any words she is not confident to attempt, and carry on to the end of the piece of writing. You can then go back over the writing with your child reading and you providing the spellings.
- ❑ When helping your child with spelling, use the 'Look, cover, write' method shown below for words she should be able to spell. Write more difficult words for her.

> ### Look, cover, write
>
> Children learn spellings by forming a picture in their heads. Try this method:
>
> - ✧ Write the word down in small letters on a piece of paper.
> - ✧ Allow your child to look at it for as long as she wishes.
> - ✧ Cover the word while she tries to write it down on the same piece of paper.
> - ✧ Compare the words, pointing out the letters your child has got right.
> - ✧ Cover both words and try again.
>
> Repeat until the word is spelled correctly.

MATHEMATICS

In order for children to become successful at Mathematics, they need to be able to make mistakes without having them corrected every time. They will learn confidence through trying things out and using mistakes as a way of learning more. Try not to keep correcting!

In the home

- ❑ Encourage your child to help with:
  - ✧ laying the table
  - ✧ pairing socks
  - ✧ sorting toys into groups when tidying (eg all fluffy toys together, all wooden toys together)
  - ✧ putting things in order of size (eg cereals in the cupboard)
  - ✧ all aspects of cooking, especially weighing and measuring liquids

- ✧ DIY jobs, even if she just watches what is being done and has it explained to her

- ❑ Play games such as:
  - ✧ board games involving dice or counting (eg Snakes and Ladders/Ludo/Monopoly)
  - ✧ traditional card games (such as Whist)
  - ✧ card games such as Snap or Happy Families
  - ✧ dominoes

- ❑ Make sure your child has:
  - ✧ Lego and other construction toys
  - ✧ a calculator to experiment and play with

Shopping

- ❑ Talk to your child about:
  - ✧ the cost of different things
  - ✧ how things are packaged so that as many as possible can fit on a shelf
  - ✧ the different types of measures (eg lemonade comes in litres, butter in grammes, shoe sizes)
  - ✧ coins and notes

- ❑ Encourage your child to:
  - ✧ read prices and quantities for you
  - ✧ guess how much the shopping will amount to
  - ✧ pay for things
  - ✧ work out simple change needed

On journeys

❏ Encourage your child to:

   ✧ count things like paving stones, steps, red cars, with you and on her own

   ✧ look out for signs saying how many miles you still have to travel

   ✧ watch the petrol pump display turning at the petrol station

   ✧ tell you what speed you are doing (if she has sight of the speedometer)

   ✧ count how many stops there are on the bus or the tube from looking at the map

On day trips and holidays

❏ Share with your child:

   ✧ looking at maps and routes

   ✧ talking about best ways of getting somewhere

   ✧ how much the holiday or trip will cost

   ✧ 24-hour time

   ✧ flight times and delays

   ✧ how seats are numbered on coaches and planes

   ✧ how much food you need to take

❏ Encourage your child to:

   ✧ use pocket money wisely (or to accept that it has gone if she doesn't)

   ✧ guess how long the journey will take, once there are some clues (we have 4 stops left/ the first 50 miles took us 1 hour)

   ✧ help you plan the holiday or trip

SCIENCE

Science is about finding out about the world around us: learning how it works and why things happen, and experimenting to gather more information. Most of your child's Science understanding will come from being encouraged to ask questions about the world we live in.

❏ Talk to your child about:

   ✧ why we need food

   ✧ why we need exercise

   ✧ the different parts of the body and what we need them for

   ✧ the weather

   ✧ the seasons

   ✧ animals, and how they are the same or different from us

   ✧ human babies and animal babies

   ✧ plants, and what they need to grow

   ✧ how things work

   ✧ what things are made of, and why

❏ Encourage your child to:

   ✧ grow different plants indoors (eg daffodil, cress)

   ✧ have her own plot in the garden to grow plants

   ✧ make moving toys (using Meccano or Lego Technic)

   ✧ look for small creatures in the garden, in the pond, by the sea

   ✧ use a magnifying glass to look closely at small things

❏ Take your child to:

   ✧ the Science Museum in London

   ✧ any good, interactive museums

   ✧ zoos, especially interactive zoos

   ✧ the seaside

   ✧ the countryside

   ✧ wildlife centres

   ✧ forests and woods

INFORMATION TECHNOLOGY

Most parents think that information technology means computers. However, all of the following are examples of information technology; telephones of all sorts, radio and television, teletext, video cameras and recorders, still and polaroid cameras, calculators, electronic organisers, stereos, as well as anything which uses a computer chip such as washing machines and dishwashers. Talk to your child about how these things work.

If you use a computer or word processor at home, explain what it can do and allow her to use it.

If you have a multi-media computer, buy one of the educational CD-ROMs on a subject she is interested in, such as Microsoft's *Dinosaurs*, *Oceans* or *Dangerous Creatures*, or Dorling Kindersley's *How Things Work* and use them together to find out information.

DESIGN TECHNOLOGY

Design technology is all about how things work and why they are designed in that way. It includes 'food technology' and incorporates various materials from metal to fabric.

❑ Encourage your child to
  ◇ look at bridges and structures and ask why they were constructed that way
  ◇ look at bicycles and see how they work
  ◇ look at the different ways wheels are attached to toy cars
  ◇ take apart simple things that are about to be thrown away such as spring action ball-point pens to see how they work (you need to be safety conscious here and do this with her)
  ◇ talk about mechanical things and how they work
  ◇ cook together, paying particular attention to why certain ingredients are used
  ◇ make things such as pencil cases out of fabric and see which stitches are best for holding together, which are best for decoration

HISTORY AND GEOGRAPHY

❑ Encourage your child to:
  ◇ tell you how to get home from familiar places
  ◇ help to navigate on journeys
  ◇ look at atlases, maps and globes
  ◇ use simple encyclopaedias or CD-ROMs
  ◇ look at old-fashioned objects and compare them with new ones
  ◇ watch television programmes set in history

❑ Talk to your child about:
  ◇ the difference between past, present and future
  ◇ how things were different when you were young
  ◇ the history of your family (make a simple family tree)
  ◇ the history of your house (if you know it)
  ◇ other parts of this country and other countries of the world (particularly if you have relatives in other parts of the country or the world)
  ◇ continents, countries, seas and oceans using a globe and/or world map.
  ◇ physical features such as mountains, rivers, valleys and sea
  ◇ the history and location of areas you visit on holiday

❑ Take your child to:
- ✧ local museums as well as famous museums
- ✧ children's theatre
- ✧ ancient ruins
- ✧ landscapes which are different to that of your home area

ART

In the home

Encourage your child to:
- ✧ use different types of paper, scissors and glue to make things, paint and draw
- ✧ draw with pencils, wax crayons, chalks, paints, felt pens
- ✧ use different brushes to paint; fine, flat and large
- ✧ experiment with colour and design
- ✧ build models with boxes
- ✧ make flat and 3-D designs with modelling materials such as plasticine

Outside

❑ Help your child to see:
- ✧ the changing patterns and colours in the landscape, the sky, trees
- ✧ the beauty of townscapes, especially when merged with nature (during a sunset, when long shadows are cast)
- ✧ beautiful things (a perfect shell, a small leaf, a butterfly, the petals of a daisy)
- ✧ ugly things (rubbish, dereliction, etc.)

❑ Take your child to:
- ✧ art galleries or art or photographic exhibitions
- ✧ parks or anywhere where there are large sculptures
- ✧ craft demonstrations

MUSIC

❑ Encourage your child to:
- ✧ sing without fear of rebuke
- ✧ make music on real or toy instruments
- ✧ beat time using home made shakers or drums while music is played
- ✧ create simple tunes or rhythms
- ✧ enjoy listening to a range of music, including classical
- ✧ sing simple songs with you
- ✧ take up an instrument (schools often provide lessons for various instruments although there is usually a charge for this)

❑ Take your child to:
- ✧ short performances of live music, such as orchestral music, choral works, individual musicians, pop and jazz
- ✧ concerts for children; most concert halls provide these
- ✧ carol singing venues

PHYSICAL EDUCATION

❑ Encourage your child to:
- ✧ play outside in safe areas
- ✧ take part in group sports, such as rounders, football etc.
- ✧ go swimming regularly
- ✧ run races
- ✧ play games with the family in the garden or park or on the beach
- ✧ take part in family activities such as ten-pin bowling or mini golf
- ✧ use climbing frames and other play furniture in the park
- ✧ join young versions of youth organisations such as 'Beavers' or 'Rainbows' (the very junior sections of Scouts and Guides)

Getting involved with the school

There are a large number of ways in which you can get involved with your child's school. However, this does require time and commitment. If you have little time, helping on trips out or with Parent-Teacher Association activities is a way to make a contribution. If you have more time, you might be able to help in class on a regular basis, or stand for election as a governor of the school or an officer of the Parent-Teacher Association.

The following are all ways you can help:

PARENTS' ASSOCIATIONS

Most schools have organisations of parents and staff. They can be called PTAs (Parent-Teacher Associations), PSAs (Parent-Staff Associations), Friends or school associations but they all consist of a committee and helpers. These people run the social events at the school, and in so doing raise money for the school. To get involved approach any committee member or ask at the school office.

The National Confederation of Parent Teacher Associations (NCPTA) promotes partnership between parents, teachers and all those involved in children's education. See the inside front cover of this book for details.

HELPING AT SCHOOL

Most teachers welcome regular help in the classroom. A helper might be asked to sit with a group of children to ensure that they play a game correctly, share a book with a child or help with dressing/undressing for swimming or PE. If you would rather not help in class, there are many other jobs you can do such as helping in the library or getting equipment ready for lessons. However, if you want to help in this way you must be able to go to the school regularly when it is convenient for the teacher, and your presence in class should not affect your child in any way.

If you cannot help regularly, you might consider helping out on school visits. When children are taken out of school, even on a local visit, several adults need to go with them for safety reasons. Ask your child's teacher if s/he needs this type of help.

BECOMING A GOVERNOR

Schools are run by governors in much the same way as companies are run by directors. It is necessary for several of the governors to be parents at the school in order to represent parents' views. Elections are held every 4 years and only the parents of the children at the school can vote. Any parent can stand for election at this time.

A governor of a school is a responsible position which requires considerable amounts of time with no pay. You will be expected to be involved fully in the life of the school and attend committee and full governors' meetings several times a year. Of all the ways of getting involved in your child's school, this is the most demanding but perhaps the most satisfying.

ATTENDING MEETINGS AND EVENTS

Even if you cannot spare the time to be an organiser of events, your attendance will show your support for the school and help you get involved. Meetings are equally important. If you do not have the time to be a governor, attendance at the annual meetings which governors hold with parents will enable you to find out more about the school. Plays, class assemblies and concerts all give you an insight into the school. You will probably attend performances your child is involved in, but if you also go to performances by older children you will gain more insight into the school and see what you can expect as your child gets older.

Going on to junior or middle school

Children move from Key Stage 1 to Key Stage 2 in the school year during which they are 8. If your child is in a primary school there will be little change in that he will progress through the same school. However, there will be a change in the work he does, because there is a different curriculum in Key Stage 2. The subjects are the same, but there is far more factual knowledge to be learned.

If your child is at an infant school, he will also have to change school at this time. Often the infant school is linked with a junior school and transfer is automatic. In some cases, however, you will have to apply for a place at the junior school of your choice. Your child's school should advise you if this is the case.

If your child is at a first school, he will begin his Key Stage 2 curriculum at the first school and complete it at a middle school. Usually, several first schools feed a middle school and transfer is automatic. Sometimes you will have to opt for a school of your choice.

Even if transfer to a junior or middle school is automatic, this does not affect your right to choose an alternative school. However, you should think carefully about this as the transfer will be far less traumatic for your child if he is moving with all his friends.

There should be arrangements for your child to visit his new school and for teachers to exchange information. You also need to get to know the new school.

◇ Read the school prospectus.
◇ Make sure you attend 'new parent' meetings.
◇ Take advantage of any chance to visit the new school for open events such as fairs and open days.
◇ Read the results of the last school inspection.

About the Authors

Shirley Clarke is one of the UK's foremost primary assessment consultants and Barry Silsby is a head teacher

Useful addresses

Christian Education Movement
Royal Buildings
Victoria Street
Derby DE1 1GW

Tel: 01332 296655

Commission for Racial Equality
Elliot House
10–12 Allington Street
London SW1E 5EH

Tel: 0171 828 7022

Curriculum and Assessment Authority for Wales
Suite 2
Castle Buildings
Womanby Street
Cardiff CF1 9SX

Tel: 01222 375400

Department for Education and Employment
Sanctuary Buildings
Great Smith Street
London SW1P 3BT

Tel: 0171 925 5000

Department for Education and Employment Publications Centre
PO Box 6927
London E3 3NZ

Tel: 0171 925 5000

Equal Opportunities Commission
Overseas House
Quay Street
Manchester M3 3HN

Tel: 0161 833 9244

General Synod Board of Education
Church House
Great Smith Street
London SW1P 3NZ

Tel: 0171 222 9011

Grant Maintained Schools Foundation
36 Great Smith Street
London SW1P 3BU

Tel: 0171 233 4666

Her Majesty's Stationery Office Publications Centre
PO Box 276
London SW8 5DT

Tel: 0171 873 0011

Independent Schools Information Service
56 Buckingham Gate
London SW1E 6AG

Tel: 0171 630 8793

Kidscape Stop Bullying
152 Buckingham Palace Road
London SW1W 9TR

Tel: 0171 730 3300

National Association for Gifted Children
Park Campus
Boughton Green Road
Northampton NN2 7AL

Tel: 01604 792300

National Confederation of Parent Teacher Associations (NCPTA)
2 Ebbsfield Estate
Stonebridge Road
Gravesend DA11 9DZ

Tel: 01474 560618

ISBN 0 340 69353 3

Text copyright © 1997
Shirley Clarke and Barry Silsby

Illustrations copyright © 1997
Sascha Lipscomb

The rights of Shirley Clarke and Barry Silsby to be identified as the authors of this work have been asserted by them in accordance with the Copyright, Design and Patents Act 1988.

First published in Great Britain 1997

10 9 8 7 6 5 4 3 2 1

Published by Hodder Children's Books, a division of Hodder Headline plc, 338 Euston Road, London NW1 3BH

Printed and bound in Great Britain

A CIP record is registered by and held at the British Library.